Wild Soul Movement presents:
POWER 2019

ELIZABETH DIALTO

Copyright © 2018 Elizabeth DiAlto
All rights reserved. No part of this book may be reproduced in any form without permission in writing from the author. Reviewers may quote brief passages in reviews.
ISBN: 9781790931200

This POWER 2019 Journal Belongs to:

_____

If found, please contact me at:

_____

Powerful one,

For many years I had an aching desire that I couldn't identify inside of me. At times I thought it was for the love of a partner until I finally realized it was to know myself intimately and truly, trust myself completely and love myself deeply. This is the best feeling in the world. It's from this place that we can anchor in our POWER and to live truthfully and meaningfully.

The times we are living in ESPECIALLY call us to do this and I'm so grateful you decided to take this journey with me in 2019.

Home is not a place.

Everything you've ever needed has ALWAYS been inside of you.

You deserve to feel deep love, peace, calm, joy, pleasure, and adoration from within.

Follow me through these pages and you will.

xo,

Elizabeth

THE WILD SOUL WOMAN MANIFESTO

An invitation to live into, a practice, a dedication, a pledge.

I am a woman, not a lovelier version of a man.

I am devoted to loving myself in the untamed way – through cultivating self-acceptance, awareness, knowledge, respect, and trust. I am committed to discovering and living into my ever-evolving truth. The truth of what it means to be a woman in the 21st century. The truth of what it means to be me, the me that I AM, not that society, culture, family, government, religion or other structures have dictated to me. I am discerning.

I listen to my wild soul and trust her innate wisdom and guidance.

I have boundaries. I do not sacrifice myself for the benefit of others. I say no when I mean no and yes when I mean yes. I am just as worthy of my own time, energy, and attention as all of my loved ones. I am a loved one. I do not need others to be different or agree with me for me to feel OK. I do my best to respect others' beliefs, opinions, cultures, choices, self-expression, and sexuality, even if I don't understand. I am a global sister. I am a safe place to land for all life and all people. I know that it's not all about me, but that it does start with me and I happily accept responsibility for my own life.

I am a work in progress and a work of art.

My body is sacred. I am willing to have courageous conversations. I embrace my uniqueness, my power, my beauty, my creativity, my inner fire, my passion, my fierceness and my softness.

I reserve the right to change my mind.

When I want to be harsh with myself I choose gentleness instead. I honor the earth and all her creations. I am unashamed. I trust that my temporary circumstances never have to be my permanent reality. I am a powerful creator. I am receptive. I am a force for expansion, for love, and for good.

I am a Wild Soul Woman.

I hereby pledge to do my best and work towards embodying this manifesto in 2019.

Print Name: _____

Signature: _____

CONTENTS

January..1
February..5
March..9
April..13
May..17
June..21
July..25
August..29
September..33
October..37
November.. 41
December.. 45
Daily Power Pages..49

JANUARY
Surrender + Release

CHECKLIST (check box once completed):

- ☐ Surrender + Release Video Lesson
- ☐ Surrender + Release Guided Visualization
- ☐ Journal reflections for the mantra
- ☐ Wild Soul Movement Practice Video for the mantra (indicate how many times you did it) _____

Notes: Write down any helpful thoughts or ideas you have throughout the month about maintaining "holy consistency" with the materials.

MANTRA: It is safe to for me to let go of what no longer serves me

Important: The emphasis of this mantra is on feeling safe to let go. It's a preparation mantra (you'll notice each new topic begins with one). I am not asking you to do any letting go yet, just inviting you to consider what might not serve you.

REFLECTION: What people, places, and stuff are you holding on to that no longer serve you? (These can range from long-term relationships to minor stuff like your junk drawer. It all takes up space. Don't think too much, just free write).

How do you visualize space? Blank paper? Clean sheets? Open field? Sun? Sky? Mountains? Earth? Open water? (Recommendation: Hold onto whatever image of space you love best and feel most connected and imagine it growing inside of you as you prepare to release the things that aren't serving you during your movement practices this month.)

FEBRUARY
Surrender + Release

CHECKLIST (check box once completed):

- ☐ Surrender + Release Video Lesson
- ☐ Surrender + Release Guided Visualization
- ☐ Journal reflections for the mantra
- ☐ Wild Soul Movement Practice Video for the mantra (indicate how many times you did it) _____

Notes: Write down any helpful thoughts or ideas you have throughout the month about maintaining "holy consistency" with the materials.

MANTRA: I release with compassion and forgiveness

REFLECTION: For each thing you wrote on your list last month, write below, "I release [insert thing] with compassion and forgiveness." And remember, forgiveness happens in layers over time. So even if you're not ready to completely release or forgive, you're chipping away at it and that is progress!

MARCH
Surrender + Release

CHECKLIST (check box once completed):

- ☐ Surrender + Release Video Lesson
- ☐ Surrender + Release Guided Visualization
- ☐ Journal reflections for the mantra
- ☐ Wild Soul Movement Practice Video for the mantra (indicate how many times you did it) _____

Notes: Write down any helpful thoughts or ideas you have throughout the month about maintaining "holy consistency" with the materials.

MANTRA: Less control, more magic

REFLECTION: What are the things you cling to? Grasp for? Try your hardest to control?

What do you gain personally from controlling these things? How does it make you feel?

Now that you've identified the feelings you seek to derive from controlling things, what are other ways you can pursue these feelings without having to control anything?

APRIL
Trust + Receptivity

CHECKLIST (check box once completed):

- ☐ Trust + Receptivity Video Lesson
- ☐ Trust + Receptivity Guided Visualization
- ☐ Journal reflections for the mantra
- ☐ Wild Soul Movement Practice Video for the mantra (indicate how many times you did it) _____

Notes: Write down any helpful thoughts or ideas you have throughout the month about maintaining "holy consistency" with the materials.

MANTRA: It is safe for me to trust myself

REFLECTION: When we don't trust Life to support us, we inadvertently put up energetic blocks to receiving. Many of us were taught growing up not to trust ourselves, that authority was outside of us, and that other people always/often know better than we do for ourselves. It's time to create a new belief system and habits to support it.

When or where did you learn not to trust? Whose voice is in your head delivering that message? (example, mom, dad, other relative, teacher, friend...etc.)

Can you remember any times when you ignored your gut instincts and ended up kicking yourself for it? List them here.

In the space below, rewrite some or all of the stories as if you had chosen to listen to your gut...this will help to replace any bitter emotions or resentment and elicit the practice of trusting your intuition.

MAY
Trust + Receptivity

CHECKLIST (check box once completed):

- ☐ Trust + Receptivity Video Lesson
- ☐ Trust + Receptivity Guided Visualization
- ☐ Journal reflections for the mantra
- ☐ Wild Soul Movement Practice Video for the mantra (indicate how many times you did it) _____

Notes: Write down any helpful thoughts or ideas you have throughout the month about maintaining "holy consistency" with the materials.

MANTRA: I am open and receptive

REFLECTION: Take all of the blank space below and list out EVERY SINGLE possible thing you can appreciate about yourself. If you need thought joggers consider the things people thank you for most often? Things that come naturally to you? Any compliments you've been given recently? Anything you secretly or not so secretly like when you look in the mirror? Be generous with yourself and brag it up here.

How does that feel? Was it easy? Hard? Did you want to judge yourself or play down your strengths? Did you discover some things you really loved?

JUNE
Trust + Receptivity

CHECKLIST (check box once completed):

- ☐ Trust + Receptivity Video Lesson
- ☐ Trust + Receptivity Guided Visualization
- ☐ Journal reflections for the mantra
- ☐ Wild Soul Movement Practice Video for the mantra (indicate how many times you did it) _____

Notes: Write down any helpful thoughts or ideas you have throughout the month about maintaining "holy consistency" with the materials.

MANTRA: Divine grace blesses and surrounds me at all times

REFLECTION: List 50-100 things in your life RIGHT now that you're grateful for. Can be small things like "my pillows" "coffee" "lotion" or more meaningful things like "the way the light dances on the wall in my bedroom close to sunset." (Note, this is different from the self-appreciations we did last month, but feel free to include yourself on this list!)

List 3-5 things that have been really challenging in your life in the last few years. Next to them, write down any blessings you can think of that came from them, even though the times were hard and even painful.

JULY
Wild Dreaming + Desire

CHECKLIST (check box once completed):

- ☐ Wild Dreaming + Desire Video Lesson
- ☐ Wild Dreaming + Desire Guided Visualization
- ☐ Journal reflections for the mantra
- ☐ Wild Soul Movement Practice Video for the mantra (indicate how many times you did it) _____

Notes: Write down any helpful thoughts or ideas you have throughout the month about maintaining "holy consistency" with the materials.

MANTRA: It is safe for me to dream wildly

REFLECTION: What were your dreams when you were a child? If you have trouble remembering here are some thought joggers: what were your favorite games to play? Toys? Movies? TV Shows? Who or what did you want to be when you grew up? Alternatively, is there someone you can ask who was around during your childhood, friends, family, etc.? It's ok to ask them, "Hey, do you remember what I wanted to be when I grew up? Or any dreams I'd talk about as a kid?"

Can you remember WHY you wanted or enjoyed these things?

What are your dreams now?

Why do you want these things?

AUGUST
Wild Dreaming + Desire

CHECKLIST (check box once completed):

- ☐ Wild Dreaming + Desire Video Lesson
- ☐ Wild Dreaming + Desire Guided Visualization
- ☐ Journal reflections for the mantra
- ☐ Wild Soul Movement Practice Video for the mantra (indicate how many times you did it) _____

Notes: Write down any helpful thoughts or ideas you have throughout the month about maintaining "holy consistency" with the materials.

MANTRA: I trust and align with the holy desires of my soul

REFLECTION: Last month you listed your dreams. Dreams are the MACRO - big picture. Desires are the MICRO - the smaller wants that are the building blocks to your dreams.

So what are your desires? Think in terms of how you want to feel, act, be, and live in the world? How do you want to show up in life? Think about people you admire? What do you admire about them? Those are desires peeking through. A friend once told me "Your Spirit speaks through you by means of your desires." They're little whispers that guide you along the way, inviting you "Follow me, I'm the truth." So, get them all on paper here...

Similar to your dreams, answer WHY? Why these desires? If there's too many to answer every one, pick your top 3-5.

SEPTEMBER
Wild Dreaming + Desire

CHECKLIST (check box once completed):

- ☐ Wild Dreaming + Desire Video Lesson
- ☐ Wild Dreaming + Desire Guided Visualization
- ☐ Journal reflections for the mantra
- ☐ Wild Soul Movement Practice Video for the mantra (indicate how many times you did it) _____

Notes: Write down any helpful thoughts or ideas you have throughout the month about maintaining "holy consistency" with the materials.

MANTRA: I am worthy of success beyond my imagining

REFLECTION: Take a look back at your dream list from July, write down your top 3 below. Then, look at your desire list from August and underneath each dream, write down the desire that matches it. (It's ok if some of them repeat).

Now, answer "What could success beyond my imagining look and feel like to me?" (I get that this is a little paradoxical since it's beyond your imagining, but play along…it still works.)

What actions can you take each day to get closer to your desires and therefore your dreams as well?

Inspired action tells the Universe "I trust you and I know I'm worthy." Look back over the last several months in this journal - is there more to let go of? Space to create? Forgiveness that needs to happen? Can you move more? Love more? Really commit to a daily appreciation practice? Identify which things make you FEEL like you are moving forward towards what you want.

What we focus on expands. It's time to focus on the things you want and deserve. YES.

OCTOBER
Love + Truth

CHECKLIST (check box once completed):

- ☐ Love + Truth Video Lesson
- ☐ Love + Truth Guided Visualization
- ☐ Journal reflections for the mantra
- ☐ Wild Soul Movement Practice Video for the mantra (indicate how many times you did it) _____

Notes: Write down any helpful thoughts or ideas you have throughout the month about maintaining "holy consistency" with the materials.

MANTRA: It is safe for me to live in and from my truth

REFLECTION: Without overthinking it, write down what you believe your current values to be.

Without overthinking it, write down what your priorities are.

Now that you're a bit more clear on your values and priorities, below write down some truths for you. If it helps, you can categorize them under health, wealth, relationships and self-mastery/spirituality.

NOVEMBER
Love + Truth

CHECKLIST (check box once completed):

- ☐ Love + Truth Video Lesson
- ☐ Love + Truth Guided Visualization
- ☐ Journal reflections for the mantra
- ☐ Wild Soul Movement Practice Video for the mantra (indicate how many times you did it) _____

Notes: Write down any helpful thoughts or ideas you have throughout the month about maintaining "holy consistency" with the materials.

MANTRA: I am love, courage, compassion and wisdom embodied

REFLECTION: Love: What does it mean to you? How does it make you feel? Where do you have it in spades? Where do you want more of it?

Courage: What does it mean to you? How does it make you feel? Where do you have it in spades? Where do you want more of it?

Compassion: What does it mean to you? How does it make you feel? Where do you have it in spades? Where do you want more of it?

Wisdom: What does it mean to you? How does it make you feel? Where do you have it in spades? Where do you want more of it?

DECEMBER
Love + Truth

CHECKLIST (check box once completed):

- ☐ Love + Truth Video Lesson
- ☐ Love + Truth Guided Visualization
- ☐ Journal reflections for the mantra
- ☐ Wild Soul Movement Practice Video for the mantra (indicate how many times you did it) _____

Notes: Write down any helpful thoughts or ideas you have throughout the month about maintaining "holy consistency" with the materials.

MANTRA: I use my power for expansion, for love and for good

REFLECTION: What have your beliefs been about power up until now? What has it looked like in your life traditionally? Who has it? Who doesn't? Is it dangerous? Safe? Healthy? Unhealthy?

What are your beliefs about power now?

When do you feel the most powerful? And what actions can you take to continue cultivating this power?

DAILY POWER PAGES

The second half of the journal is extra space for reflection, appreciation, insights and more.

DATE: _____
TOPIC: _____
MANTRA: _____

Appreciations (for life, self, POWER, the people in your life, anything else):

Other reflection (thoughts, feelings, insights, musings, aha's, questions to ask on Q+As, etc.):

DATE: _____
TOPIC: _____
MANTRA: _____

Appreciations (for life, self, POWER, the people in your life, anything else):

Other reflection (thoughts, feelings, insights, musings, aha's, questions to ask on Q+As, etc.):

DATE: _____
TOPIC: _____
MANTRA: _____

Appreciations (for life, self, POWER, the people in your life, anything else):

Other reflection (thoughts, feelings, insights, musings, aha's, questions to ask on Q+As, etc.):

DATE: _____
TOPIC: _____
MANTRA: _____

Appreciations (for life, self, POWER, the people in your life, anything else):

Other reflection (thoughts, feelings, insights, musings, aha's, questions to ask on Q+As, etc.):

DATE: _____
TOPIC: _____
MANTRA: _____

Appreciations (for life, self, POWER, the people in your life, anything else):

Other reflection (thoughts, feelings, insights, musings, aha's, questions to ask on Q+As, etc.):

DATE: _____
TOPIC: _____
MANTRA: _____

Appreciations (for life, self, POWER, the people in your life, anything else):

Other reflection (thoughts, feelings, insights, musings, aha's, questions to ask on Q+As, etc.):

DATE: _____
TOPIC: _____
MANTRA: _____

Appreciations (for life, self, POWER, the people in your life, anything else):

```
┌─────────────────────────────────────────────────┐
│                                                 │
│                                                 │
│                                                 │
│                                                 │
│                                                 │
│                                                 │
│                                                 │
│                                                 │
└─────────────────────────────────────────────────┘
```

Other reflection (thoughts, feelings, insights, musings, aha's, questions to ask on Q+As, etc.):

```
┌─────────────────────────────────────────────────┐
│                                                 │
│                                                 │
│                                                 │
│                                                 │
│                                                 │
│                                                 │
│                                                 │
│                                                 │
└─────────────────────────────────────────────────┘
```

DATE: _____
TOPIC: _____
MANTRA: _____

Appreciations (for life, self, POWER, the people in your life, anything else):

Other reflection (thoughts, feelings, insights, musings, aha's, questions to ask on Q+As, etc.):

DATE: _____
TOPIC: _____
MANTRA: _____

Appreciations (for life, self, POWER, the people in your life, anything else):

Other reflection (thoughts, feelings, insights, musings, aha's, questions to ask on Q+As, etc.):

DATE: _____
TOPIC: _____
MANTRA: _____

Appreciations (for life, self, POWER, the people in your life, anything else):

Other reflection (thoughts, feelings, insights, musings, aha's, questions to ask on Q+As, etc.):

DATE: _____
TOPIC: _____
MANTRA: _____

Appreciations (for life, self, POWER, the people in your life, anything else):

Other reflection (thoughts, feelings, insights, musings, aha's, questions to ask on Q+As, etc.):

DATE: _____
TOPIC: _____
MANTRA: _____

Appreciations (for life, self, POWER, the people in your life, anything else):

Other reflection (thoughts, feelings, insights, musings, aha's, questions to ask on Q+As, etc.):

DATE: _____
TOPIC: _____
MANTRA: _____

Appreciations (for life, self, POWER, the people in your life, anything else):

Other reflection (thoughts, feelings, insights, musings, aha's, questions to ask on Q+As, etc.):

DATE: _____
TOPIC: _____
MANTRA: _____

Appreciations (for life, self, POWER, the people in your life, anything else):

Other reflection (thoughts, feelings, insights, musings, aha's, questions to ask on Q+As, etc.):

DATE: _____
TOPIC: _____
MANTRA: _____

Appreciations (for life, self, POWER, the people in your life, anything else):

[   ]

Other reflection (thoughts, feelings, insights, musings, aha's, questions to ask on Q+As, etc.):

[   ]

DATE: _____
TOPIC: _____
MANTRA: _____

Appreciations (for life, self, POWER, the people in your life, anything else):

Other reflection (thoughts, feelings, insights, musings, aha's, questions to ask on Q+As, etc.):

DATE: _____
TOPIC: _____
MANTRA: _____

Appreciations (for life, self, POWER, the people in your life, anything else):

Other reflection (thoughts, feelings, insights, musings, aha's, questions to ask on Q+As, etc.):

DATE: _____
TOPIC: _____
MANTRA: _____

Appreciations (for life, self, POWER, the people in your life, anything else):

Other reflection (thoughts, feelings, insights, musings, aha's, questions to ask on Q+As, etc.):

DATE: _____
TOPIC: _____
MANTRA: _____

Appreciations (for life, self, POWER, the people in your life, anything else):

Other reflection (thoughts, feelings, insights, musings, aha's, questions to ask on Q+As, etc.):

DATE: _____
TOPIC: _____
MANTRA: _____

Appreciations (for life, self, POWER, the people in your life, anything else):

```
┌─────────────────────────────────────────────────────────────┐
│                                                             │
│                                                             │
│                                                             │
│                                                             │
│                                                             │
│                                                             │
│                                                             │
│                                                             │
└─────────────────────────────────────────────────────────────┘
```

Other reflection (thoughts, feelings, insights, musings, aha's, questions to ask on Q+As, etc.):

```
┌─────────────────────────────────────────────────────────────┐
│                                                             │
│                                                             │
│                                                             │
│                                                             │
│                                                             │
│                                                             │
│                                                             │
│                                                             │
└─────────────────────────────────────────────────────────────┘
```

DATE: _____
TOPIC: _____
MANTRA: _____

Appreciations (for life, self, POWER, the people in your life, anything else):

Other reflection (thoughts, feelings, insights, musings, aha's, questions to ask on Q+As, etc.):

DATE: _____
TOPIC: _____
MANTRA: _____

Appreciations (for life, self, POWER, the people in your life, anything else):

Other reflection (thoughts, feelings, insights, musings, aha's, questions to ask on Q+As, etc.):

DATE: _____
TOPIC: _____
MANTRA: _____

Appreciations (for life, self, POWER, the people in your life, anything else):

Other reflection (thoughts, feelings, insights, musings, aha's, questions to ask on Q+As, etc.):

DATE: _____
TOPIC: _____
MANTRA: _____

Appreciations (for life, self, POWER, the people in your life, anything else):

Other reflection (thoughts, feelings, insights, musings, aha's, questions to ask on Q+As, etc.):

DATE: _____
TOPIC: _____
MANTRA: _____

Appreciations (for life, self, POWER, the people in your life, anything else):

Other reflection (thoughts, feelings, insights, musings, aha's, questions to ask on Q+As, etc.):

DATE: _____
TOPIC: _____
MANTRA: _____

Appreciations (for life, self, POWER, the people in your life, anything else):

Other reflection (thoughts, feelings, insights, musings, aha's, questions to ask on Q+As, etc.):

DATE: _____
TOPIC: _____
MANTRA: _____

Appreciations (for life, self, POWER, the people in your life, anything else):

Other reflection (thoughts, feelings, insights, musings, aha's, questions to ask on Q+As, etc.):

DATE: _____
TOPIC: _____
MANTRA: _____

Appreciations (for life, self, POWER, the people in your life, anything else):

Other reflection (thoughts, feelings, insights, musings, aha's, questions to ask on Q+As, etc.):

DATE: _____
TOPIC: _____
MANTRA: _____

Appreciations (for life, self, POWER, the people in your life, anything else):

Other reflection (thoughts, feelings, insights, musings, aha's, questions to ask on Q+As, etc.):

DATE: _____
TOPIC: _____
MANTRA: _____

Appreciations (for life, self, POWER, the people in your life, anything else):

Other reflection (thoughts, feelings, insights, musings, aha's, questions to ask on Q+As, etc.):

DATE: _____
TOPIC: _____
MANTRA: _____

Appreciations (for life, self, POWER, the people in your life, anything else):

Other reflection (thoughts, feelings, insights, musings, aha's, questions to ask on Q+As, etc.):

DATE: _____
TOPIC: _____
MANTRA: _____

Appreciations (for life, self, POWER, the people in your life, anything else):

Other reflection (thoughts, feelings, insights, musings, aha's, questions to ask on Q+As, etc.):

DATE: _____
TOPIC: _____
MANTRA: _____

Appreciations (for life, self, POWER, the people in your life, anything else):

Other reflection (thoughts, feelings, insights, musings, aha's, questions to ask on Q+As, etc.):

DATE: _____
TOPIC: _____
MANTRA: _____

Appreciations (for life, self, POWER, the people in your life, anything else):

Other reflection (thoughts, feelings, insights, musings, aha's, questions to ask on Q+As, etc.):

DATE: _____
TOPIC: _____
MANTRA: _____

Appreciations (for life, self, POWER, the people in your life, anything else):

```
┌─────────────────────────────────────────────────────────┐
│                                                         │
│                                                         │
│                                                         │
│                                                         │
│                                                         │
│                                                         │
└─────────────────────────────────────────────────────────┘
```

Other reflection (thoughts, feelings, insights, musings, aha's, questions to ask on Q+As, etc.):

```
┌─────────────────────────────────────────────────────────┐
│                                                         │
│                                                         │
│                                                         │
│                                                         │
│                                                         │
│                                                         │
└─────────────────────────────────────────────────────────┘
```

DATE: _____
TOPIC: _____
MANTRA: _____

Appreciations (for life, self, POWER, the people in your life, anything else):

```
┌─────────────────────────────────────────────────┐
│                                                 │
│                                                 │
│                                                 │
│                                                 │
│                                                 │
│                                                 │
│                                                 │
└─────────────────────────────────────────────────┘
```

Other reflection (thoughts, feelings, insights, musings, aha's, questions to ask on Q+As, etc.):

```
┌─────────────────────────────────────────────────┐
│                                                 │
│                                                 │
│                                                 │
│                                                 │
│                                                 │
│                                                 │
│                                                 │
└─────────────────────────────────────────────────┘
```

DATE: _____
TOPIC: _____
MANTRA: _____

Appreciations (for life, self, POWER, the people in your life, anything else):

Other reflection (thoughts, feelings, insights, musings, aha's, questions to ask on Q+As, etc.):

DATE: _____
TOPIC: _____
MANTRA: _____

Appreciations (for life, self, POWER, the people in your life, anything else):

Other reflection (thoughts, feelings, insights, musings, aha's, questions to ask on Q+As, etc.):

DATE: _____
TOPIC: _____
MANTRA: _____

Appreciations (for life, self, POWER, the people in your life, anything else):

Other reflection (thoughts, feelings, insights, musings, aha's, questions to ask on Q+As, etc.):

DATE: _____
TOPIC: _____
MANTRA: _____

Appreciations (for life, self, POWER, the people in your life, anything else):

Other reflection (thoughts, feelings, insights, musings, aha's, questions to ask on Q+As, etc.):

DATE: _____
TOPIC: _____
MANTRA: _____

Appreciations (for life, self, POWER, the people in your life, anything else):

[   ]

Other reflection (thoughts, feelings, insights, musings, aha's, questions to ask on Q+As, etc.):

[   ]

DATE: _____
TOPIC: _____
MANTRA: _____

Appreciations (for life, self, POWER, the people in your life, anything else):

Other reflection (thoughts, feelings, insights, musings, aha's, questions to ask on Q+As, etc.):

DATE: _____
TOPIC: _____
MANTRA: _____

Appreciations (for life, self, POWER, the people in your life, anything else):

Other reflection (thoughts, feelings, insights, musings, aha's, questions to ask on Q+As, etc.):

DATE: _____
TOPIC: _____
MANTRA: _____

Appreciations (for life, self, POWER, the people in your life, anything else):

Other reflection (thoughts, feelings, insights, musings, aha's, questions to ask on Q+As, etc.):

DATE: _____
TOPIC: _____
MANTRA: _____

Appreciations (for life, self, POWER, the people in your life, anything else):

Other reflection (thoughts, feelings, insights, musings, aha's, questions to ask on Q+As, etc.):

DATE: _____
TOPIC: _____
MANTRA: _____

Appreciations (for life, self, POWER, the people in your life, anything else):

```
┌─────────────────────────────────────────────────────────┐
│                                                         │
│                                                         │
│                                                         │
│                                                         │
│                                                         │
│                                                         │
│                                                         │
└─────────────────────────────────────────────────────────┘
```

Other reflection (thoughts, feelings, insights, musings, aha's, questions to ask on Q+As, etc.):

```
┌─────────────────────────────────────────────────────────┐
│                                                         │
│                                                         │
│                                                         │
│                                                         │
│                                                         │
│                                                         │
│                                                         │
└─────────────────────────────────────────────────────────┘
```

DATE: _____
TOPIC: _____
MANTRA: _____

Appreciations (for life, self, POWER, the people in your life, anything else):

Other reflection (thoughts, feelings, insights, musings, aha's, questions to ask on Q+As, etc.):

DATE: _____
TOPIC: _____
MANTRA: _____

Appreciations (for life, self, POWER, the people in your life, anything else):

Other reflection (thoughts, feelings, insights, musings, aha's, questions to ask on Q+As, etc.):

DATE: _____
TOPIC: _____
MANTRA: _____

Appreciations (for life, self, POWER, the people in your life, anything else):

Other reflection (thoughts, feelings, insights, musings, aha's, questions to ask on Q+As, etc.):

DATE: _____
TOPIC: _____
MANTRA: _____

Appreciations (for life, self, POWER, the people in your life, anything else):

Other reflection (thoughts, feelings, insights, musings, aha's, questions to ask on Q+As, etc.):

DATE: _____
TOPIC: _____
MANTRA: _____

Appreciations (for life, self, POWER, the people in your life, anything else):

Other reflection (thoughts, feelings, insights, musings, aha's, questions to ask on Q+As, etc.):

DATE: _____
TOPIC: _____
MANTRA: _____

Appreciations (for life, self, POWER, the people in your life, anything else):

Other reflection (thoughts, feelings, insights, musings, aha's, questions to ask on Q+As, etc.):

DATE: _____
TOPIC: _____
MANTRA: _____

Appreciations (for life, self, POWER, the people in your life, anything else):

```
┌─────────────────────────────────────────────────────┐
│                                                     │
│                                                     │
│                                                     │
│                                                     │
│                                                     │
│                                                     │
│                                                     │
│                                                     │
└─────────────────────────────────────────────────────┘
```

Other reflection (thoughts, feelings, insights, musings, aha's, questions to ask on Q+As, etc.):

```
┌─────────────────────────────────────────────────────┐
│                                                     │
│                                                     │
│                                                     │
│                                                     │
│                                                     │
│                                                     │
│                                                     │
│                                                     │
└─────────────────────────────────────────────────────┘
```

DATE: _____
TOPIC: _____
MANTRA: _____

Appreciations (for life, self, POWER, the people in your life, anything else):

Other reflection (thoughts, feelings, insights, musings, aha's, questions to ask on Q+As, etc.):

DATE: _____
TOPIC: _____
MANTRA: _____

Appreciations (for life, self, POWER, the people in your life, anything else):

Other reflection (thoughts, feelings, insights, musings, aha's, questions to ask on Q+As, etc.):

DATE: _____
TOPIC: _____
MANTRA: _____

Appreciations (for life, self, POWER, the people in your life, anything else):

Other reflection (thoughts, feelings, insights, musings, aha's, questions to ask on Q+As, etc.):

DATE: _____
TOPIC: _____
MANTRA: _____

Appreciations (for life, self, POWER, the people in your life, anything else):

[   ]

Other reflection (thoughts, feelings, insights, musings, aha's, questions to ask on Q+As, etc.):

[   ]

DATE: _____
TOPIC: _____
MANTRA: _____

Appreciations (for life, self, POWER, the people in your life, anything else):

Other reflection (thoughts, feelings, insights, musings, aha's, questions to ask on Q+As, etc.):

DATE: _____
TOPIC: _____
MANTRA: _____

Appreciations (for life, self, POWER, the people in your life, anything else):

Other reflection (thoughts, feelings, insights, musings, aha's, questions to ask on Q+As, etc.):

DATE: _____
TOPIC: _____
MANTRA: _____

Appreciations (for life, self, POWER, the people in your life, anything else):

Other reflection (thoughts, feelings, insights, musings, aha's, questions to ask on Q+As, etc.):

DATE: _____
TOPIC: _____
MANTRA: _____

Appreciations (for life, self, POWER, the people in your life, anything else):

Other reflection (thoughts, feelings, insights, musings, aha's, questions to ask on Q+As, etc.):

DATE: _____
TOPIC: _____
MANTRA: _____

Appreciations (for life, self, POWER, the people in your life, anything else):

Other reflection (thoughts, feelings, insights, musings, aha's, questions to ask on Q+As, etc.):

DATE: _____
TOPIC: _____
MANTRA: _____

Appreciations (for life, self, POWER, the people in your life, anything else):

Other reflection (thoughts, feelings, insights, musings, aha's, questions to ask on Q+As, etc.):

DATE: _____
TOPIC: _____
MANTRA: _____

Appreciations (for life, self, POWER, the people in your life, anything else):

Other reflection (thoughts, feelings, insights, musings, aha's, questions to ask on Q+As, etc.):

DATE: _____
TOPIC: _____
MANTRA: _____

Appreciations (for life, self, POWER, the people in your life, anything else):

Other reflection (thoughts, feelings, insights, musings, aha's, questions to ask on Q+As, etc.):

DATE: _____
TOPIC: _____
MANTRA: _____

Appreciations (for life, self, POWER, the people in your life, anything else):

Other reflection (thoughts, feelings, insights, musings, aha's, questions to ask on Q+As, etc.):

DATE: _____
TOPIC: _____
MANTRA: _____

Appreciations (for life, self, POWER, the people in your life, anything else):

Other reflection (thoughts, feelings, insights, musings, aha's, questions to ask on Q+As, etc.):

DATE: _____
TOPIC: _____
MANTRA: _____

Appreciations (for life, self, POWER, the people in your life, anything else):

Other reflection (thoughts, feelings, insights, musings, aha's, questions to ask on Q+As, etc.):

DATE: _____
TOPIC: _____
MANTRA: _____

Appreciations (for life, self, POWER, the people in your life, anything else):

Other reflection (thoughts, feelings, insights, musings, aha's, questions to ask on Q+As, etc.):

DATE: _____
TOPIC: _____
MANTRA: _____

Appreciations (for life, self, POWER, the people in your life, anything else):

Other reflection (thoughts, feelings, insights, musings, aha's, questions to ask on Q+As, etc.):

DATE: _____
TOPIC: _____
MANTRA: _____

Appreciations (for life, self, POWER, the people in your life, anything else):

[   ]

Other reflection (thoughts, feelings, insights, musings, aha's, questions to ask on Q+As, etc.):

[   ]

DATE: _____
TOPIC: _____
MANTRA: _____

Appreciations (for life, self, POWER, the people in your life, anything else):

```
┌─────────────────────────────────────────────────────────────┐
│                                                             │
│                                                             │
│                                                             │
│                                                             │
│                                                             │
│                                                             │
│                                                             │
└─────────────────────────────────────────────────────────────┘
```

Other reflection (thoughts, feelings, insights, musings, aha's, questions to ask on Q+As, etc.):

```
┌─────────────────────────────────────────────────────────────┐
│                                                             │
│                                                             │
│                                                             │
│                                                             │
│                                                             │
│                                                             │
│                                                             │
└─────────────────────────────────────────────────────────────┘
```

DATE: _____
TOPIC: _____
MANTRA: _____

Appreciations (for life, self, POWER, the people in your life, anything else):

Other reflection (thoughts, feelings, insights, musings, aha's, questions to ask on Q+As, etc.):

DATE: _____
TOPIC: _____
MANTRA: _____

Appreciations (for life, self, POWER, the people in your life, anything else):

Other reflection (thoughts, feelings, insights, musings, aha's, questions to ask on Q+As, etc.):

DATE: _____
TOPIC: _____
MANTRA: _____

Appreciations (for life, self, POWER, the people in your life, anything else):

Other reflection (thoughts, feelings, insights, musings, aha's, questions to ask on Q+As, etc.):

DATE: _____
TOPIC: _____
MANTRA: _____

Appreciations (for life, self, POWER, the people in your life, anything else):

Other reflection (thoughts, feelings, insights, musings, aha's, questions to ask on Q+As, etc.):

DATE: _____
TOPIC: _____
MANTRA: _____

Appreciations (for life, self, POWER, the people in your life, anything else):

```
┌─────────────────────────────────────────────────┐
│                                                 │
│                                                 │
│                                                 │
│                                                 │
│                                                 │
│                                                 │
└─────────────────────────────────────────────────┘
```

Other reflection (thoughts, feelings, insights, musings, aha's, questions to ask on Q+As, etc.):

```
┌─────────────────────────────────────────────────┐
│                                                 │
│                                                 │
│                                                 │
│                                                 │
│                                                 │
│                                                 │
└─────────────────────────────────────────────────┘
```

DATE: _____
TOPIC: _____
MANTRA: _____

Appreciations (for life, self, POWER, the people in your life, anything else):

Other reflection (thoughts, feelings, insights, musings, aha's, questions to ask on Q+As, etc.):

DATE: _____
TOPIC: _____
MANTRA: _____

Appreciations (for life, self, POWER, the people in your life, anything else):

Other reflection (thoughts, feelings, insights, musings, aha's, questions to ask on Q+As, etc.):

DATE: _____
TOPIC: _____
MANTRA: _____

Appreciations (for life, self, POWER, the people in your life, anything else):

[   ]

Other reflection (thoughts, feelings, insights, musings, aha's, questions to ask on Q+As, etc.):

[   ]

DATE: _____
TOPIC: _____
MANTRA: _____

Appreciations (for life, self, POWER, the people in your life, anything else):

Other reflection (thoughts, feelings, insights, musings, aha's, questions to ask on Q+As, etc.):

DATE: _____
TOPIC: _____
MANTRA: _____

Appreciations (for life, self, POWER, the people in your life, anything else):

Other reflection (thoughts, feelings, insights, musings, aha's, questions to ask on Q+As, etc.):

DATE: _____
TOPIC: _____
MANTRA: _____

Appreciations (for life, self, POWER, the people in your life, anything else):

[   ]

Other reflection (thoughts, feelings, insights, musings, aha's, questions to ask on Q+As, etc.):

[   ]

DATE: _____
TOPIC: _____
MANTRA: _____

Appreciations (for life, self, POWER, the people in your life, anything else):

```
┌─────────────────────────────────────────────────┐
│                                                 │
│                                                 │
│                                                 │
│                                                 │
│                                                 │
│                                                 │
│                                                 │
└─────────────────────────────────────────────────┘
```

Other reflection (thoughts, feelings, insights, musings, aha's, questions to ask on Q+As, etc.):

```
┌─────────────────────────────────────────────────┐
│                                                 │
│                                                 │
│                                                 │
│                                                 │
│                                                 │
│                                                 │
│                                                 │
└─────────────────────────────────────────────────┘
```

DATE: _____
TOPIC: _____
MANTRA: _____

Appreciations (for life, self, POWER, the people in your life, anything else):

Other reflection (thoughts, feelings, insights, musings, aha's, questions to ask on Q+As, etc.):

DATE: _____
TOPIC: _____
MANTRA: _____

Appreciations (for life, self, POWER, the people in your life, anything else):

```
┌─────────────────────────────────────────────────────────┐
│                                                         │
│                                                         │
│                                                         │
│                                                         │
│                                                         │
│                                                         │
│                                                         │
└─────────────────────────────────────────────────────────┘
```

Other reflection (thoughts, feelings, insights, musings, aha's, questions to ask on Q+As, etc.):

```
┌─────────────────────────────────────────────────────────┐
│                                                         │
│                                                         │
│                                                         │
│                                                         │
│                                                         │
│                                                         │
│                                                         │
└─────────────────────────────────────────────────────────┘
```

DATE: _____
TOPIC: _____
MANTRA: _____

Appreciations (for life, self, POWER, the people in your life, anything else):

Other reflection (thoughts, feelings, insights, musings, aha's, questions to ask on Q+As, etc.):

DATE: _____
TOPIC: _____
MANTRA: _____

Appreciations (for life, self, POWER, the people in your life, anything else):

Other reflection (thoughts, feelings, insights, musings, aha's, questions to ask on Q+As, etc.):

DATE: _____
TOPIC: _____
MANTRA: _____

Appreciations (for life, self, POWER, the people in your life, anything else):

[   ]

Other reflection (thoughts, feelings, insights, musings, aha's, questions to ask on Q+As, etc.):

[   ]

DATE: _____
TOPIC: _____
MANTRA: _____

Appreciations (for life, self, POWER, the people in your life, anything else):

```
┌─────────────────────────────────────────────────────────┐
│                                                         │
│                                                         │
│                                                         │
│                                                         │
│                                                         │
│                                                         │
└─────────────────────────────────────────────────────────┘
```

Other reflection (thoughts, feelings, insights, musings, aha's, questions to ask on Q+As, etc.):

```
┌─────────────────────────────────────────────────────────┐
│                                                         │
│                                                         │
│                                                         │
│                                                         │
│                                                         │
│                                                         │
└─────────────────────────────────────────────────────────┘
```

DATE: _____
TOPIC: _____
MANTRA: _____

Appreciations (for life, self, POWER, the people in your life, anything else):

Other reflection (thoughts, feelings, insights, musings, aha's, questions to ask on Q+As, etc.):

DATE: _____
TOPIC: _____
MANTRA: _____

Appreciations (for life, self, POWER, the people in your life, anything else):

Other reflection (thoughts, feelings, insights, musings, aha's, questions to ask on Q+As, etc.):

DATE: _____
TOPIC: _____
MANTRA: _____

Appreciations (for life, self, POWER, the people in your life, anything else):

Other reflection (thoughts, feelings, insights, musings, aha's, questions to ask on Q+As, etc.):

DATE: _____
TOPIC: _____
MANTRA: _____

Appreciations (for life, self, POWER, the people in your life, anything else):

Other reflection (thoughts, feelings, insights, musings, aha's, questions to ask on Q+As, etc.):

DATE: _____
TOPIC: _____
MANTRA: _____

Appreciations (for life, self, POWER, the people in your life, anything else):

```
┌─────────────────────────────────────────────┐
│                                             │
│                                             │
│                                             │
│                                             │
│                                             │
│                                             │
└─────────────────────────────────────────────┘
```

Other reflection (thoughts, feelings, insights, musings, aha's, questions to ask on Q+As, etc.):

```
┌─────────────────────────────────────────────┐
│                                             │
│                                             │
│                                             │
│                                             │
│                                             │
│                                             │
└─────────────────────────────────────────────┘
```

DATE: _____
TOPIC: _____
MANTRA: _____

Appreciations (for life, self, POWER, the people in your life, anything else):

```
┌─────────────────────────────────────────────────────────┐
│                                                         │
│                                                         │
│                                                         │
│                                                         │
│                                                         │
│                                                         │
└─────────────────────────────────────────────────────────┘
```

Other reflection (thoughts, feelings, insights, musings, aha's, questions to ask on Q+As, etc.):

```
┌─────────────────────────────────────────────────────────┐
│                                                         │
│                                                         │
│                                                         │
│                                                         │
│                                                         │
│                                                         │
└─────────────────────────────────────────────────────────┘
```

DATE: _____
TOPIC: _____
MANTRA: _____

Appreciations (for life, self, POWER, the people in your life, anything else):

[   ]

Other reflection (thoughts, feelings, insights, musings, aha's, questions to ask on Q+As, etc.):

[   ]

DATE: _____
TOPIC: _____
MANTRA: _____

Appreciations (for life, self, POWER, the people in your life, anything else):

Other reflection (thoughts, feelings, insights, musings, aha's, questions to ask on Q+As, etc.):

DATE: _____
TOPIC: _____
MANTRA: _____

Appreciations (for life, self, POWER, the people in your life, anything else):

Other reflection (thoughts, feelings, insights, musings, aha's, questions to ask on Q+As, etc.):

DATE: _____
TOPIC: _____
MANTRA: _____

Appreciations (for life, self, POWER, the people in your life, anything else):

Other reflection (thoughts, feelings, insights, musings, aha's, questions to ask on Q+As, etc.):

DATE: _____
TOPIC: _____
MANTRA: _____

Appreciations (for life, self, POWER, the people in your life, anything else):

Other reflection (thoughts, feelings, insights, musings, aha's, questions to ask on Q+As, etc.):

DATE: _____
TOPIC: _____
MANTRA: _____

Appreciations (for life, self, POWER, the people in your life, anything else):

[   ]

Other reflection (thoughts, feelings, insights, musings, aha's, questions to ask on Q+As, etc.):

[   ]

DATE: _____
TOPIC: _____
MANTRA: _____

Appreciations (for life, self, POWER, the people in your life, anything else):

Other reflection (thoughts, feelings, insights, musings, aha's, questions to ask on Q+As, etc.):

DATE: _____
TOPIC: _____
MANTRA: _____

Appreciations (for life, self, POWER, the people in your life, anything else):

Other reflection (thoughts, feelings, insights, musings, aha's, questions to ask on Q+As, etc.):

DATE: _____
TOPIC: _____
MANTRA: _____

Appreciations (for life, self, POWER, the people in your life, anything else):

Other reflection (thoughts, feelings, insights, musings, aha's, questions to ask on Q+As, etc.):

DATE: _____
TOPIC: _____
MANTRA: _____

Appreciations (for life, self, POWER, the people in your life, anything else):

Other reflection (thoughts, feelings, insights, musings, aha's, questions to ask on Q+As, etc.):

DATE: _____
TOPIC: _____
MANTRA: _____

Appreciations (for life, self, POWER, the people in your life, anything else):

Other reflection (thoughts, feelings, insights, musings, aha's, questions to ask on Q+As, etc.):

DATE: _____
TOPIC: _____
MANTRA: _____

Appreciations (for life, self, POWER, the people in your life, anything else):

Other reflection (thoughts, feelings, insights, musings, aha's, questions to ask on Q+As, etc.):

DATE: _____
TOPIC: _____
MANTRA: _____

Appreciations (for life, self, POWER, the people in your life, anything else):

Other reflection (thoughts, feelings, insights, musings, aha's, questions to ask on Q+As, etc.):

DATE: _____
TOPIC: _____
MANTRA: _____

Appreciations (for life, self, POWER, the people in your life, anything else):

Other reflection (thoughts, feelings, insights, musings, aha's, questions to ask on Q+As, etc.):

DATE: _____
TOPIC: _____
MANTRA: _____

Appreciations (for life, self, POWER, the people in your life, anything else):

Other reflection (thoughts, feelings, insights, musings, aha's, questions to ask on Q+As, etc.):

DATE: _____
TOPIC: _____
MANTRA: _____

Appreciations (for life, self, POWER, the people in your life, anything else):

Other reflection (thoughts, feelings, insights, musings, aha's, questions to ask on Q+As, etc.):

DATE: _____
TOPIC: _____
MANTRA: _____

Appreciations (for life, self, POWER, the people in your life, anything else):

[   ]

Other reflection (thoughts, feelings, insights, musings, aha's, questions to ask on Q+As, etc.):

[   ]

DATE: _____
TOPIC: _____
MANTRA: _____

Appreciations (for life, self, POWER, the people in your life, anything else):

Other reflection (thoughts, feelings, insights, musings, aha's, questions to ask on Q+As, etc.):

DATE: _____
TOPIC: _____
MANTRA: _____

Appreciations (for life, self, POWER, the people in your life, anything else):

Other reflection (thoughts, feelings, insights, musings, aha's, questions to ask on Q+As, etc.):

DATE: _____
TOPIC: _____
MANTRA: _____

Appreciations (for life, self, POWER, the people in your life, anything else):

Other reflection (thoughts, feelings, insights, musings, aha's, questions to ask on Q+As, etc.):

DATE: _____
TOPIC: _____
MANTRA: _____

Appreciations (for life, self, POWER, the people in your life, anything else):

Other reflection (thoughts, feelings, insights, musings, aha's, questions to ask on Q+As, etc.):

DATE: _____
TOPIC: _____
MANTRA: _____

Appreciations (for life, self, POWER, the people in your life, anything else):

Other reflection (thoughts, feelings, insights, musings, aha's, questions to ask on Q+As, etc.):

DATE: _____
TOPIC: _____
MANTRA: _____

Appreciations (for life, self, POWER, the people in your life, anything else):

Other reflection (thoughts, feelings, insights, musings, aha's, questions to ask on Q+As, etc.):

DATE: _____
TOPIC: _____
MANTRA: _____

Appreciations (for life, self, POWER, the people in your life, anything else):

Other reflection (thoughts, feelings, insights, musings, aha's, questions to ask on Q+As, etc.):

DATE: _____
TOPIC: _____
MANTRA: _____

Appreciations (for life, self, POWER, the people in your life, anything else):

```
```

Other reflection (thoughts, feelings, insights, musings, aha's, questions to ask on Q+As, etc.):

DATE: _____
TOPIC: _____
MANTRA: _____

Appreciations (for life, self, POWER, the people in your life, anything else):

Other reflection (thoughts, feelings, insights, musings, aha's, questions to ask on Q+As, etc.):

DATE: _____
TOPIC: _____
MANTRA: _____

Appreciations (for life, self, POWER, the people in your life, anything else):

```
┌─────────────────────────────────────────────┐
│                                             │
│                                             │
│                                             │
│                                             │
│                                             │
│                                             │
│                                             │
└─────────────────────────────────────────────┘
```

Other reflection (thoughts, feelings, insights, musings, aha's, questions to ask on Q+As, etc.):

```
┌─────────────────────────────────────────────┐
│                                             │
│                                             │
│                                             │
│                                             │
│                                             │
│                                             │
│                                             │
└─────────────────────────────────────────────┘
```

DATE: _____
TOPIC: _____
MANTRA: _____

Appreciations (for life, self, POWER, the people in your life, anything else):

Other reflection (thoughts, feelings, insights, musings, aha's, questions to ask on Q+As, etc.):

DATE: _____
TOPIC: _____
MANTRA: _____

Appreciations (for life, self, POWER, the people in your life, anything else):

Other reflection (thoughts, feelings, insights, musings, aha's, questions to ask on Q+As, etc.):

DATE: _____
TOPIC: _____
MANTRA: _____

Appreciations (for life, self, POWER, the people in your life, anything else):

```
[                                                                    ]
```

Other reflection (thoughts, feelings, insights, musings, aha's, questions to ask on Q+As, etc.):

```
[                                                                    ]
```

DATE: _____
TOPIC: _____
MANTRA: _____

Appreciations (for life, self, POWER, the people in your life, anything else):

Other reflection (thoughts, feelings, insights, musings, aha's, questions to ask on Q+As, etc.):

DATE: _____
TOPIC: _____
MANTRA: _____

Appreciations (for life, self, POWER, the people in your life, anything else):

Other reflection (thoughts, feelings, insights, musings, aha's, questions to ask on Q+As, etc.):

DATE: _____
TOPIC: _____
MANTRA: _____

Appreciations (for life, self, POWER, the people in your life, anything else):

Other reflection (thoughts, feelings, insights, musings, aha's, questions to ask on Q+As, etc.):

DATE: _____
TOPIC: _____
MANTRA: _____

Appreciations (for life, self, POWER, the people in your life, anything else):

Other reflection (thoughts, feelings, insights, musings, aha's, questions to ask on Q+As, etc.):

DATE: _____
TOPIC: _____
MANTRA: _____

Appreciations (for life, self, POWER, the people in your life, anything else):

Other reflection (thoughts, feelings, insights, musings, aha's, questions to ask on Q+As, etc.):

DATE: _____
TOPIC: _____
MANTRA: _____

Appreciations (for life, self, POWER, the people in your life, anything else):

Other reflection (thoughts, feelings, insights, musings, aha's, questions to ask on Q+As, etc.):

DATE: _____
TOPIC: _____
MANTRA: _____

Appreciations (for life, self, POWER, the people in your life, anything else):

Other reflection (thoughts, feelings, insights, musings, aha's, questions to ask on Q+As, etc.):

DATE: _____
TOPIC: _____
MANTRA: _____

Appreciations (for life, self, POWER, the people in your life, anything else):

Other reflection (thoughts, feelings, insights, musings, aha's, questions to ask on Q+As, etc.):

DATE: _____
TOPIC: _____
MANTRA: _____

Appreciations (for life, self, POWER, the people in your life, anything else):

Other reflection (thoughts, feelings, insights, musings, aha's, questions to ask on Q+As, etc.):

DATE: _____
TOPIC: _____
MANTRA: _____

Appreciations (for life, self, POWER, the people in your life, anything else):

Other reflection (thoughts, feelings, insights, musings, aha's, questions to ask on Q+As, etc.):

DATE: _____
TOPIC: _____
MANTRA: _____

Appreciations (for life, self, POWER, the people in your life, anything else):

Other reflection (thoughts, feelings, insights, musings, aha's, questions to ask on Q+As, etc.):

DATE: _____
TOPIC: _____
MANTRA: _____

Appreciations (for life, self, POWER, the people in your life, anything else):

Other reflection (thoughts, feelings, insights, musings, aha's, questions to ask on Q+As, etc.):

DATE: _____
TOPIC: _____
MANTRA: _____

Appreciations (for life, self, POWER, the people in your life, anything else):

Other reflection (thoughts, feelings, insights, musings, aha's, questions to ask on Q+As, etc.):

DATE: _____
TOPIC: _____
MANTRA: _____

Appreciations (for life, self, POWER, the people in your life, anything else):

Other reflection (thoughts, feelings, insights, musings, aha's, questions to ask on Q+As, etc.):

DATE: _____
TOPIC: _____
MANTRA: _____

Appreciations (for life, self, POWER, the people in your life, anything else):

Other reflection (thoughts, feelings, insights, musings, aha's, questions to ask on Q+As, etc.):

DATE: _____
TOPIC: _____
MANTRA: _____

Appreciations (for life, self, POWER, the people in your life, anything else):

```
┌─────────────────────────────────────────────────────────────┐
│                                                             │
│                                                             │
│                                                             │
│                                                             │
│                                                             │
│                                                             │
│                                                             │
└─────────────────────────────────────────────────────────────┘
```

Other reflection (thoughts, feelings, insights, musings, aha's, questions to ask on Q+As, etc.):

```
┌─────────────────────────────────────────────────────────────┐
│                                                             │
│                                                             │
│                                                             │
│                                                             │
│                                                             │
│                                                             │
│                                                             │
└─────────────────────────────────────────────────────────────┘
```

DATE: _____
TOPIC: _____
MANTRA: _____

Appreciations (for life, self, POWER, the people in your life, anything else):

Other reflection (thoughts, feelings, insights, musings, aha's, questions to ask on Q+As, etc.):

DATE: _____
TOPIC: _____
MANTRA: _____

Appreciations (for life, self, POWER, the people in your life, anything else):

Other reflection (thoughts, feelings, insights, musings, aha's, questions to ask on Q+As, etc.):

DATE: _____
TOPIC: _____
MANTRA: _____

Appreciations (for life, self, POWER, the people in your life, anything else):

Other reflection (thoughts, feelings, insights, musings, aha's, questions to ask on Q+As, etc.):

DATE: _____
TOPIC: _____
MANTRA: _____

Appreciations (for life, self, POWER, the people in your life, anything else):

Other reflection (thoughts, feelings, insights, musings, aha's, questions to ask on Q+As, etc.):

DATE: _____
TOPIC: _____
MANTRA: _____

Appreciations (for life, self, POWER, the people in your life, anything else):

[   ]

Other reflection (thoughts, feelings, insights, musings, aha's, questions to ask on Q+As, etc.):

[   ]

DATE: _____
TOPIC: _____
MANTRA: _____

Appreciations (for life, self, POWER, the people in your life, anything else):

[   ]

Other reflection (thoughts, feelings, insights, musings, aha's, questions to ask on Q+As, etc.):

[   ]

DATE: _____
TOPIC: _____
MANTRA: _____

Appreciations (for life, self, POWER, the people in your life, anything else):

Other reflection (thoughts, feelings, insights, musings, aha's, questions to ask on Q+As, etc.):

DATE: _____
TOPIC: _____
MANTRA: _____

Appreciations (for life, self, POWER, the people in your life, anything else):

Other reflection (thoughts, feelings, insights, musings, aha's, questions to ask on Q+As, etc.):

DATE: _____
TOPIC: _____
MANTRA: _____

Appreciations (for life, self, POWER, the people in your life, anything else):

Other reflection (thoughts, feelings, insights, musings, aha's, questions to ask on Q+As, etc.):

DATE: _____
TOPIC: _____
MANTRA: _____

Appreciations (for life, self, POWER, the people in your life, anything else):

Other reflection (thoughts, feelings, insights, musings, aha's, questions to ask on Q+As, etc.):

DATE: _____
TOPIC: _____
MANTRA: _____

Appreciations (for life, self, POWER, the people in your life, anything else):

Other reflection (thoughts, feelings, insights, musings, aha's, questions to ask on Q+As, etc.):

DATE: _____
TOPIC: _____
MANTRA: _____

Appreciations (for life, self, POWER, the people in your life, anything else):

Other reflection (thoughts, feelings, insights, musings, aha's, questions to ask on Q+As, etc.):

DATE: _____
TOPIC: _____
MANTRA: _____

Appreciations (for life, self, POWER, the people in your life, anything else):

Other reflection (thoughts, feelings, insights, musings, aha's, questions to ask on Q+As, etc.):

DATE: _____
TOPIC: _____
MANTRA: _____

Appreciations (for life, self, POWER, the people in your life, anything else):

Other reflection (thoughts, feelings, insights, musings, aha's, questions to ask on Q+As, etc.):

DATE: _____
TOPIC: _____
MANTRA: _____

Appreciations (for life, self, POWER, the people in your life, anything else):

Other reflection (thoughts, feelings, insights, musings, aha's, questions to ask on Q+As, etc.):

DATE: _____
TOPIC: _____
MANTRA: _____

Appreciations (for life, self, POWER, the people in your life, anything else):

Other reflection (thoughts, feelings, insights, musings, aha's, questions to ask on Q+As, etc.):

DATE: _____
TOPIC: _____
MANTRA: _____

Appreciations (for life, self, POWER, the people in your life, anything else):

Other reflection (thoughts, feelings, insights, musings, aha's, questions to ask on Q+As, etc.):

DATE: _____
TOPIC: _____
MANTRA: _____

Appreciations (for life, self, POWER, the people in your life, anything else):

Other reflection (thoughts, feelings, insights, musings, aha's, questions to ask on Q+As, etc.):

DATE: _____
TOPIC: _____
MANTRA: _____

Appreciations (for life, self, POWER, the people in your life, anything else):

Other reflection (thoughts, feelings, insights, musings, aha's, questions to ask on Q+As, etc.):

DATE: _____
TOPIC: _____
MANTRA: _____

Appreciations (for life, self, POWER, the people in your life, anything else):

Other reflection (thoughts, feelings, insights, musings, aha's, questions to ask on Q+As, etc.):

DATE: _____
TOPIC: _____
MANTRA: _____

Appreciations (for life, self, POWER, the people in your life, anything else):

[   ]

Other reflection (thoughts, feelings, insights, musings, aha's, questions to ask on Q+As, etc.):

[   ]

DATE: _____
TOPIC: _____
MANTRA: _____

Appreciations (for life, self, POWER, the people in your life, anything else):

Other reflection (thoughts, feelings, insights, musings, aha's, questions to ask on Q+As, etc.):

DATE: _____
TOPIC: _____
MANTRA: _____

Appreciations (for life, self, POWER, the people in your life, anything else):

Other reflection (thoughts, feelings, insights, musings, aha's, questions to ask on Q+As, etc.):

DATE: _____
TOPIC: _____
MANTRA: _____

Appreciations (for life, self, POWER, the people in your life, anything else):

Other reflection (thoughts, feelings, insights, musings, aha's, questions to ask on Q+As, etc.):

DATE: _____
TOPIC: _____
MANTRA: _____

Appreciations (for life, self, POWER, the people in your life, anything else):

```
┌─────────────────────────────────────────────────────┐
│                                                     │
│                                                     │
│                                                     │
│                                                     │
│                                                     │
│                                                     │
└─────────────────────────────────────────────────────┘
```

Other reflection (thoughts, feelings, insights, musings, aha's, questions to ask on Q+As, etc.):

```
┌─────────────────────────────────────────────────────┐
│                                                     │
│                                                     │
│                                                     │
│                                                     │
│                                                     │
│                                                     │
└─────────────────────────────────────────────────────┘
```

DATE: _____
TOPIC: _____
MANTRA: _____

Appreciations (for life, self, POWER, the people in your life, anything else):

[   ]

Other reflection (thoughts, feelings, insights, musings, aha's, questions to ask on Q+As, etc.):

[   ]

DATE: _____
TOPIC: _____
MANTRA: _____

Appreciations (for life, self, POWER, the people in your life, anything else):

Other reflection (thoughts, feelings, insights, musings, aha's, questions to ask on Q+As, etc.):

DATE: _____
TOPIC: _____
MANTRA: _____

Appreciations (for life, self, POWER, the people in your life, anything else):

Other reflection (thoughts, feelings, insights, musings, aha's, questions to ask on Q+As, etc.):

DATE: _____
TOPIC: _____
MANTRA: _____

Appreciations (for life, self, POWER, the people in your life, anything else):

Other reflection (thoughts, feelings, insights, musings, aha's, questions to ask on Q+As, etc.):

DATE: _____
TOPIC: _____
MANTRA: _____

Appreciations (for life, self, POWER, the people in your life, anything else):

Other reflection (thoughts, feelings, insights, musings, aha's, questions to ask on Q+As, etc.):

DATE: _____
TOPIC: _____
MANTRA: _____

Appreciations (for life, self, POWER, the people in your life, anything else):

Other reflection (thoughts, feelings, insights, musings, aha's, questions to ask on Q+As, etc.):

DATE: _____
TOPIC: _____
MANTRA: _____

Appreciations (for life, self, POWER, the people in your life, anything else):

┌───┐
│   │
│   │
│   │
│   │
│   │
│   │
│   │
└───┘

Other reflection (thoughts, feelings, insights, musings, aha's, questions to ask on Q+As, etc.):

┌───┐
│   │
│   │
│   │
│   │
│   │
│   │
│   │
└───┘

DATE: _____
TOPIC: _____
MANTRA: _____

Appreciations (for life, self, POWER, the people in your life, anything else):

[   ]

Other reflection (thoughts, feelings, insights, musings, aha's, questions to ask on Q+As, etc.):

[   ]

DATE: _____
TOPIC: _____
MANTRA: _____

Appreciations (for life, self, POWER, the people in your life, anything else):

Other reflection (thoughts, feelings, insights, musings, aha's, questions to ask on Q+As, etc.):

DATE: _____
TOPIC: _____
MANTRA: _____

Appreciations (for life, self, POWER, the people in your life, anything else):

Other reflection (thoughts, feelings, insights, musings, aha's, questions to ask on Q+As, etc.):

DATE: _____
TOPIC: _____
MANTRA: _____

Appreciations (for life, self, POWER, the people in your life, anything else):

Other reflection (thoughts, feelings, insights, musings, aha's, questions to ask on Q+As, etc.):

DATE: _____
TOPIC: _____
MANTRA: _____

Appreciations (for life, self, POWER, the people in your life, anything else):

Other reflection (thoughts, feelings, insights, musings, aha's, questions to ask on Q+As, etc.):

DATE: _____
TOPIC: _____
MANTRA: _____

Appreciations (for life, self, POWER, the people in your life, anything else):

[ ]

Other reflection (thoughts, feelings, insights, musings, aha's, questions to ask on Q+As, etc.):

[ ]

DATE: _____
TOPIC: _____
MANTRA: _____

Appreciations (for life, self, POWER, the people in your life, anything else):

Other reflection (thoughts, feelings, insights, musings, aha's, questions to ask on Q+As, etc.):

DATE: _____
TOPIC: _____
MANTRA: _____

Appreciations (for life, self, POWER, the people in your life, anything else):

Other reflection (thoughts, feelings, insights, musings, aha's, questions to ask on Q+As, etc.):

DATE: _____
TOPIC: _____
MANTRA: _____

Appreciations (for life, self, POWER, the people in your life, anything else):

Other reflection (thoughts, feelings, insights, musings, aha's, questions to ask on Q+As, etc.):

DATE: _____

TOPIC: _____

MANTRA: _____

Appreciations (for life, self, POWER, the people in your life, anything else):

Other reflection (thoughts, feelings, insights, musings, aha's, questions to ask on Q+As, etc.):

DATE: _____
TOPIC: _____
MANTRA: _____

Appreciations (for life, self, POWER, the people in your life, anything else):

Other reflection (thoughts, feelings, insights, musings, aha's, questions to ask on Q+As, etc.):

DATE: _____
TOPIC: _____
MANTRA: _____

Appreciations (for life, self, POWER, the people in your life, anything else):

Other reflection (thoughts, feelings, insights, musings, aha's, questions to ask on Q+As, etc.):

DATE: _____
TOPIC: _____
MANTRA: _____

Appreciations (for life, self, POWER, the people in your life, anything else):

Other reflection (thoughts, feelings, insights, musings, aha's, questions to ask on Q+As, etc.):

DATE: _____
TOPIC: _____
MANTRA: _____

Appreciations (for life, self, POWER, the people in your life, anything else):

Other reflection (thoughts, feelings, insights, musings, aha's, questions to ask on Q+As, etc.):

DATE: _____
TOPIC: _____
MANTRA: _____

Appreciations (for life, self, POWER, the people in your life, anything else):

Other reflection (thoughts, feelings, insights, musings, aha's, questions to ask on Q+As, etc.):

DATE: _____
TOPIC: _____
MANTRA: _____

Appreciations (for life, self, POWER, the people in your life, anything else):

[   ]

Other reflection (thoughts, feelings, insights, musings, aha's, questions to ask on Q+As, etc.):

[   ]

DATE: _____
TOPIC: _____
MANTRA: _____

Appreciations (for life, self, POWER, the people in your life, anything else):

Other reflection (thoughts, feelings, insights, musings, aha's, questions to ask on Q+As, etc.):

DATE: _____
TOPIC: _____
MANTRA: _____

Appreciations (for life, self, POWER, the people in your life, anything else):

```
┌─────────────────────────────────────────────────────────────┐
│                                                             │
│                                                             │
│                                                             │
│                                                             │
│                                                             │
│                                                             │
│                                                             │
│                                                             │
└─────────────────────────────────────────────────────────────┘
```

Other reflection (thoughts, feelings, insights, musings, aha's, questions to ask on Q+As, etc.):

```
┌─────────────────────────────────────────────────────────────┐
│                                                             │
│                                                             │
│                                                             │
│                                                             │
│                                                             │
│                                                             │
│                                                             │
│                                                             │
└─────────────────────────────────────────────────────────────┘
```

DATE: _____
TOPIC: _____
MANTRA: _____

Appreciations (for life, self, POWER, the people in your life, anything else):

Other reflection (thoughts, feelings, insights, musings, aha's, questions to ask on Q+As, etc.):

DATE: _____
TOPIC: _____
MANTRA: _____

Appreciations (for life, self, POWER, the people in your life, anything else):

Other reflection (thoughts, feelings, insights, musings, aha's, questions to ask on Q+As, etc.):

DATE: _____
TOPIC: _____
MANTRA: _____

Appreciations (for life, self, POWER, the people in your life, anything else):

Other reflection (thoughts, feelings, insights, musings, aha's, questions to ask on Q+As, etc.):

DATE: _____
TOPIC: _____
MANTRA: _____

Appreciations (for life, self, POWER, the people in your life, anything else):

[   ]

Other reflection (thoughts, feelings, insights, musings, aha's, questions to ask on Q+As, etc.):

[   ]

DATE: _____
TOPIC: _____
MANTRA: _____

Appreciations (for life, self, POWER, the people in your life, anything else):

Other reflection (thoughts, feelings, insights, musings, aha's, questions to ask on Q+As, etc.):

DATE: _____
TOPIC: _____
MANTRA: _____

Appreciations (for life, self, POWER, the people in your life, anything else):

Other reflection (thoughts, feelings, insights, musings, aha's, questions to ask on Q+As, etc.):

DATE: _____
TOPIC: _____
MANTRA: _____

Appreciations (for life, self, POWER, the people in your life, anything else):

Other reflection (thoughts, feelings, insights, musings, aha's, questions to ask on Q+As, etc.):

DATE: _____
TOPIC: _____
MANTRA: _____

Appreciations (for life, self, POWER, the people in your life, anything else):

Other reflection (thoughts, feelings, insights, musings, aha's, questions to ask on Q+As, etc.):

DATE: _____
TOPIC: _____
MANTRA: _____

Appreciations (for life, self, POWER, the people in your life, anything else):

[   ]

Other reflection (thoughts, feelings, insights, musings, aha's, questions to ask on Q+As, etc.):

[   ]

DATE: _____
TOPIC: _____
MANTRA: _____

Appreciations (for life, self, POWER, the people in your life, anything else):

Other reflection (thoughts, feelings, insights, musings, aha's, questions to ask on Q+As, etc.):

DATE: _____
TOPIC: _____
MANTRA: _____

Appreciations (for life, self, POWER, the people in your life, anything else):

Other reflection (thoughts, feelings, insights, musings, aha's, questions to ask on Q+As, etc.):

DATE: _____
TOPIC: _____
MANTRA: _____

Appreciations (for life, self, POWER, the people in your life, anything else):

Other reflection (thoughts, feelings, insights, musings, aha's, questions to ask on Q+As, etc.):

DATE: _____
TOPIC: _____
MANTRA: _____

Appreciations (for life, self, POWER, the people in your life, anything else):

Other reflection (thoughts, feelings, insights, musings, aha's, questions to ask on Q+As, etc.):

DATE: _____
TOPIC: _____
MANTRA: _____

Appreciations (for life, self, POWER, the people in your life, anything else):

Other reflection (thoughts, feelings, insights, musings, aha's, questions to ask on Q+As, etc.):

DATE: _____
TOPIC: _____
MANTRA: _____

Appreciations (for life, self, POWER, the people in your life, anything else):

Other reflection (thoughts, feelings, insights, musings, aha's, questions to ask on Q+As, etc.):

DATE: _____
TOPIC: _____
MANTRA: _____

Appreciations (for life, self, POWER, the people in your life, anything else):

Other reflection (thoughts, feelings, insights, musings, aha's, questions to ask on Q+As, etc.):

DATE: _____
TOPIC: _____
MANTRA: _____

Appreciations (for life, self, POWER, the people in your life, anything else):

Other reflection (thoughts, feelings, insights, musings, aha's, questions to ask on Q+As, etc.):

DATE: _____
TOPIC: _____
MANTRA: _____

Appreciations (for life, self, POWER, the people in your life, anything else):

```
┌─────────────────────────────────────────────────────────────┐
│                                                             │
│                                                             │
│                                                             │
│                                                             │
│                                                             │
│                                                             │
│                                                             │
│                                                             │
└─────────────────────────────────────────────────────────────┘
```

Other reflection (thoughts, feelings, insights, musings, aha's, questions to ask on Q+As, etc.):

```
┌─────────────────────────────────────────────────────────────┐
│                                                             │
│                                                             │
│                                                             │
│                                                             │
│                                                             │
│                                                             │
│                                                             │
│                                                             │
└─────────────────────────────────────────────────────────────┘
```

DATE: _____
TOPIC: _____
MANTRA: _____

Appreciations (for life, self, POWER, the people in your life, anything else):

[   ]

Other reflection (thoughts, feelings, insights, musings, aha's, questions to ask on Q+As, etc.):

[   ]

DATE: _____
TOPIC: _____
MANTRA: _____

Appreciations (for life, self, POWER, the people in your life, anything else):

Other reflection (thoughts, feelings, insights, musings, aha's, questions to ask on Q+As, etc.):

DATE: _____
TOPIC: _____
MANTRA: _____

Appreciations (for life, self, POWER, the people in your life, anything else):

```
┌─────────────────────────────────────────────────────┐
│                                                     │
│                                                     │
│                                                     │
│                                                     │
│                                                     │
│                                                     │
│                                                     │
└─────────────────────────────────────────────────────┘
```

Other reflection (thoughts, feelings, insights, musings, aha's, questions to ask on Q+As, etc.):

```
┌─────────────────────────────────────────────────────┐
│                                                     │
│                                                     │
│                                                     │
│                                                     │
│                                                     │
│                                                     │
│                                                     │
└─────────────────────────────────────────────────────┘
```

DATE: _____
TOPIC: _____
MANTRA: _____

Appreciations (for life, self, POWER, the people in your life, anything else):

Other reflection (thoughts, feelings, insights, musings, aha's, questions to ask on Q+As, etc.):

DATE: _____
TOPIC: _____
MANTRA: _____

Appreciations (for life, self, POWER, the people in your life, anything else):

Other reflection (thoughts, feelings, insights, musings, aha's, questions to ask on Q+As, etc.):

DATE: _____
TOPIC: _____
MANTRA: _____

Appreciations (for life, self, POWER, the people in your life, anything else):

Other reflection (thoughts, feelings, insights, musings, aha's, questions to ask on Q+As, etc.):

DATE: _____
TOPIC: _____
MANTRA: _____

Appreciations (for life, self, POWER, the people in your life, anything else):

Other reflection (thoughts, feelings, insights, musings, aha's, questions to ask on Q+As, etc.):

DATE: _____
TOPIC: _____
MANTRA: _____

Appreciations (for life, self, POWER, the people in your life, anything else):

```
┌─────────────────────────────────────────────┐
│                                             │
│                                             │
│                                             │
│                                             │
│                                             │
│                                             │
│                                             │
└─────────────────────────────────────────────┘
```

Other reflection (thoughts, feelings, insights, musings, aha's, questions to ask on Q+As, etc.):

```
┌─────────────────────────────────────────────┐
│                                             │
│                                             │
│                                             │
│                                             │
│                                             │
│                                             │
│                                             │
└─────────────────────────────────────────────┘
```

DATE: _____
TOPIC: _____
MANTRA: _____

Appreciations (for life, self, POWER, the people in your life, anything else):

Other reflection (thoughts, feelings, insights, musings, aha's, questions to ask on Q+As, etc.):

DATE: _____
TOPIC: _____
MANTRA: _____

Appreciations (for life, self, POWER, the people in your life, anything else):

Other reflection (thoughts, feelings, insights, musings, aha's, questions to ask on Q+As, etc.):

DATE: _____
TOPIC: _____
MANTRA: _____

Appreciations (for life, self, POWER, the people in your life, anything else):

Other reflection (thoughts, feelings, insights, musings, aha's, questions to ask on Q+As, etc.):

DATE: _____
TOPIC: _____
MANTRA: _____

Appreciations (for life, self, POWER, the people in your life, anything else):

Other reflection (thoughts, feelings, insights, musings, aha's, questions to ask on Q+As, etc.):

DATE: _____
TOPIC: _____
MANTRA: _____

Appreciations (for life, self, POWER, the people in your life, anything else):

Other reflection (thoughts, feelings, insights, musings, aha's, questions to ask on Q+As, etc.):

DATE: _____
TOPIC: _____
MANTRA: _____

Appreciations (for life, self, POWER, the people in your life, anything else):

Other reflection (thoughts, feelings, insights, musings, aha's, questions to ask on Q+As, etc.):

DATE: _____
TOPIC: _____
MANTRA: _____

Appreciations (for life, self, POWER, the people in your life, anything else):

```
┌─────────────────────────────────────────────────────┐
│                                                     │
│                                                     │
│                                                     │
│                                                     │
│                                                     │
│                                                     │
│                                                     │
└─────────────────────────────────────────────────────┘
```

Other reflection (thoughts, feelings, insights, musings, aha's, questions to ask on Q+As, etc.):

```
┌─────────────────────────────────────────────────────┐
│                                                     │
│                                                     │
│                                                     │
│                                                     │
│                                                     │
│                                                     │
│                                                     │
└─────────────────────────────────────────────────────┘
```

DATE: _____
TOPIC: _____
MANTRA: _____

Appreciations (for life, self, POWER, the people in your life, anything else):

Other reflection (thoughts, feelings, insights, musings, aha's, questions to ask on Q+As, etc.):

DATE: _____
TOPIC: _____
MANTRA: _____

Appreciations (for life, self, POWER, the people in your life, anything else):

Other reflection (thoughts, feelings, insights, musings, aha's, questions to ask on Q+As, etc.):

DATE: _____
TOPIC: _____
MANTRA: _____

Appreciations (for life, self, POWER, the people in your life, anything else):

Other reflection (thoughts, feelings, insights, musings, aha's, questions to ask on Q+As, etc.):

DATE: _____
TOPIC: _____
MANTRA: _____

Appreciations (for life, self, POWER, the people in your life, anything else):

```
┌─────────────────────────────────────────────┐
│                                             │
│                                             │
│                                             │
│                                             │
│                                             │
│                                             │
└─────────────────────────────────────────────┘
```

Other reflection (thoughts, feelings, insights, musings, aha's, questions to ask on Q+As, etc.):

```
┌─────────────────────────────────────────────┐
│                                             │
│                                             │
│                                             │
│                                             │
│                                             │
│                                             │
└─────────────────────────────────────────────┘
```

DATE: _____
TOPIC: _____
MANTRA: _____

Appreciations (for life, self, POWER, the people in your life, anything else):

Other reflection (thoughts, feelings, insights, musings, aha's, questions to ask on Q+As, etc.):

DATE: _____
TOPIC: _____
MANTRA: _____

Appreciations (for life, self, POWER, the people in your life, anything else):

```
┌─────────────────────────────────────────────────────────┐
│                                                         │
│                                                         │
│                                                         │
│                                                         │
│                                                         │
│                                                         │
│                                                         │
└─────────────────────────────────────────────────────────┘
```

Other reflection (thoughts, feelings, insights, musings, aha's, questions to ask on Q+As, etc.):

```
┌─────────────────────────────────────────────────────────┐
│                                                         │
│                                                         │
│                                                         │
│                                                         │
│                                                         │
│                                                         │
│                                                         │
└─────────────────────────────────────────────────────────┘
```

DATE: _____
TOPIC: _____
MANTRA: _____

Appreciations (for life, self, POWER, the people in your life, anything else):

Other reflection (thoughts, feelings, insights, musings, aha's, questions to ask on Q+As, etc.):

DATE: _____
TOPIC: _____
MANTRA: _____

Appreciations (for life, self, POWER, the people in your life, anything else):

Other reflection (thoughts, feelings, insights, musings, aha's, questions to ask on Q+As, etc.):

DATE: _____
TOPIC: _____
MANTRA: _____

Appreciations (for life, self, POWER, the people in your life, anything else):

Other reflection (thoughts, feelings, insights, musings, aha's, questions to ask on Q+As, etc.):

DATE: _____
TOPIC: _____
MANTRA: _____

Appreciations (for life, self, POWER, the people in your life, anything else):

Other reflection (thoughts, feelings, insights, musings, aha's, questions to ask on Q+As, etc.):

DATE: _____
TOPIC: _____
MANTRA: _____

Appreciations (for life, self, POWER, the people in your life, anything else):

Other reflection (thoughts, feelings, insights, musings, aha's, questions to ask on Q+As, etc.):

DATE: _____
TOPIC: _____
MANTRA: _____

Appreciations (for life, self, POWER, the people in your life, anything else):

Other reflection (thoughts, feelings, insights, musings, aha's, questions to ask on Q+As, etc.):

DATE: _____
TOPIC: _____
MANTRA: _____

Appreciations (for life, self, POWER, the people in your life, anything else):

Other reflection (thoughts, feelings, insights, musings, aha's, questions to ask on Q+As, etc.):

DATE: _____
TOPIC: _____
MANTRA: _____

Appreciations (for life, self, POWER, the people in your life, anything else):

Other reflection (thoughts, feelings, insights, musings, aha's, questions to ask on Q+As, etc.):

DATE: _____
TOPIC: _____
MANTRA: _____

Appreciations (for life, self, POWER, the people in your life, anything else):

[   ]

Other reflection (thoughts, feelings, insights, musings, aha's, questions to ask on Q+As, etc.):

[   ]

DATE: _____
TOPIC: _____
MANTRA: _____

Appreciations (for life, self, POWER, the people in your life, anything else):

Other reflection (thoughts, feelings, insights, musings, aha's, questions to ask on Q+As, etc.):

DATE: _____
TOPIC: _____
MANTRA: _____

Appreciations (for life, self, POWER, the people in your life, anything else):

```
┌─────────────────────────────────────────────┐
│                                             │
│                                             │
│                                             │
│                                             │
│                                             │
│                                             │
└─────────────────────────────────────────────┘
```

Other reflection (thoughts, feelings, insights, musings, aha's, questions to ask on Q+As, etc.):

```
┌─────────────────────────────────────────────┐
│                                             │
│                                             │
│                                             │
│                                             │
│                                             │
│                                             │
└─────────────────────────────────────────────┘
```

DATE: _____
TOPIC: _____
MANTRA: _____

Appreciations (for life, self, POWER, the people in your life, anything else):

Other reflection (thoughts, feelings, insights, musings, aha's, questions to ask on Q+As, etc.):

DATE: _____
TOPIC: _____
MANTRA: _____

Appreciations (for life, self, POWER, the people in your life, anything else):

Other reflection (thoughts, feelings, insights, musings, aha's, questions to ask on Q+As, etc.):

DATE: _____
TOPIC: _____
MANTRA: _____

Appreciations (for life, self, POWER, the people in your life, anything else):

Other reflection (thoughts, feelings, insights, musings, aha's, questions to ask on Q+As, etc.):

DATE: _____
TOPIC: _____
MANTRA: _____

Appreciations (for life, self, POWER, the people in your life, anything else):

Other reflection (thoughts, feelings, insights, musings, aha's, questions to ask on Q+As, etc.):

DATE: _____
TOPIC: _____
MANTRA: _____

Appreciations (for life, self, POWER, the people in your life, anything else):

Other reflection (thoughts, feelings, insights, musings, aha's, questions to ask on Q+As, etc.):

DATE: _____
TOPIC: _____
MANTRA: _____

Appreciations (for life, self, POWER, the people in your life, anything else):

Other reflection (thoughts, feelings, insights, musings, aha's, questions to ask on Q+As, etc.):

DATE: _____
TOPIC: _____
MANTRA: _____

Appreciations (for life, self, POWER, the people in your life, anything else):

Other reflection (thoughts, feelings, insights, musings, aha's, questions to ask on Q+As, etc.):

DATE: _____
TOPIC: _____
MANTRA: _____

Appreciations (for life, self, POWER, the people in your life, anything else):

Other reflection (thoughts, feelings, insights, musings, aha's, questions to ask on Q+As, etc.):

DATE: _____
TOPIC: _____
MANTRA: _____

Appreciations (for life, self, POWER, the people in your life, anything else):

| |
| |

Other reflection (thoughts, feelings, insights, musings, aha's, questions to ask on Q+As, etc.):

| |
| |

DATE: _____
TOPIC: _____
MANTRA: _____

Appreciations (for life, self, POWER, the people in your life, anything else):

```
┌─────────────────────────────────────────────────────────┐
│                                                         │
│                                                         │
│                                                         │
│                                                         │
│                                                         │
│                                                         │
│                                                         │
└─────────────────────────────────────────────────────────┘
```

Other reflection (thoughts, feelings, insights, musings, aha's, questions to ask on Q+As, etc.):

```
┌─────────────────────────────────────────────────────────┐
│                                                         │
│                                                         │
│                                                         │
│                                                         │
│                                                         │
│                                                         │
│                                                         │
└─────────────────────────────────────────────────────────┘
```

DATE: _____
TOPIC: _____
MANTRA: _____

Appreciations (for life, self, POWER, the people in your life, anything else):

Other reflection (thoughts, feelings, insights, musings, aha's, questions to ask on Q+As, etc.):

DATE: _____
TOPIC: _____
MANTRA: _____

Appreciations (for life, self, POWER, the people in your life, anything else):

Other reflection (thoughts, feelings, insights, musings, aha's, questions to ask on Q+As, etc.):

DATE: _____
TOPIC: _____
MANTRA: _____

Appreciations (for life, self, POWER, the people in your life, anything else):

```
┌─────────────────────────────────────────────────────────┐
│                                                         │
│                                                         │
│                                                         │
│                                                         │
│                                                         │
│                                                         │
│                                                         │
└─────────────────────────────────────────────────────────┘
```

Other reflection (thoughts, feelings, insights, musings, aha's, questions to ask on Q+As, etc.):

```
┌─────────────────────────────────────────────────────────┐
│                                                         │
│                                                         │
│                                                         │
│                                                         │
│                                                         │
│                                                         │
└─────────────────────────────────────────────────────────┘
```

DATE: _____
TOPIC: _____
MANTRA: _____

Appreciations (for life, self, POWER, the people in your life, anything else):

Other reflection (thoughts, feelings, insights, musings, aha's, questions to ask on Q+As, etc.):

DATE: _____
TOPIC: _____
MANTRA: _____

Appreciations (for life, self, POWER, the people in your life, anything else):

Other reflection (thoughts, feelings, insights, musings, aha's, questions to ask on Q+As, etc.):

DATE: _____
TOPIC: _____
MANTRA: _____

Appreciations (for life, self, POWER, the people in your life, anything else):

Other reflection (thoughts, feelings, insights, musings, aha's, questions to ask on Q+As, etc.):

DATE: _____
TOPIC: _____
MANTRA: _____

Appreciations (for life, self, POWER, the people in your life, anything else):

Other reflection (thoughts, feelings, insights, musings, aha's, questions to ask on Q+As, etc.):

DATE: _____
TOPIC: _____
MANTRA: _____

Appreciations (for life, self, POWER, the people in your life, anything else):

Other reflection (thoughts, feelings, insights, musings, aha's, questions to ask on Q+As, etc.):

DATE: _____
TOPIC: _____
MANTRA: _____

Appreciations (for life, self, POWER, the people in your life, anything else):

Other reflection (thoughts, feelings, insights, musings, aha's, questions to ask on Q+As, etc.):

DATE: _____
TOPIC: _____
MANTRA: _____

Appreciations (for life, self, POWER, the people in your life, anything else):

```
┌─────────────────────────────────────────────────────────────┐
│                                                             │
│                                                             │
│                                                             │
│                                                             │
│                                                             │
│                                                             │
│                                                             │
└─────────────────────────────────────────────────────────────┘
```

Other reflection (thoughts, feelings, insights, musings, aha's, questions to ask on Q+As, etc.):

```
┌─────────────────────────────────────────────────────────────┐
│                                                             │
│                                                             │
│                                                             │
│                                                             │
│                                                             │
│                                                             │
│                                                             │
└─────────────────────────────────────────────────────────────┘
```

DATE: _____
TOPIC: _____
MANTRA: _____

Appreciations (for life, self, POWER, the people in your life, anything else):

Other reflection (thoughts, feelings, insights, musings, aha's, questions to ask on Q+As, etc.):

DATE: _____
TOPIC: _____
MANTRA: _____

Appreciations (for life, self, POWER, the people in your life, anything else):

Other reflection (thoughts, feelings, insights, musings, aha's, questions to ask on Q+As, etc.):

DATE: _____
TOPIC: _____
MANTRA: _____

Appreciations (for life, self, POWER, the people in your life, anything else):

Other reflection (thoughts, feelings, insights, musings, aha's, questions to ask on Q+As, etc.):

DATE: _____
TOPIC: _____
MANTRA: _____

Appreciations (for life, self, POWER, the people in your life, anything else):

Other reflection (thoughts, feelings, insights, musings, aha's, questions to ask on Q+As, etc.):

DATE: _____
TOPIC: _____
MANTRA: _____

Appreciations (for life, self, POWER, the people in your life, anything else):

Other reflection (thoughts, feelings, insights, musings, aha's, questions to ask on Q+As, etc.):

DATE: _____
TOPIC: _____
MANTRA: _____

Appreciations (for life, self, POWER, the people in your life, anything else):

Other reflection (thoughts, feelings, insights, musings, aha's, questions to ask on Q+As, etc.):

DATE: _____
TOPIC: _____
MANTRA: _____

Appreciations (for life, self, POWER, the people in your life, anything else):

[   ]

Other reflection (thoughts, feelings, insights, musings, aha's, questions to ask on Q+As, etc.):

[   ]

DATE: _____
TOPIC: _____
MANTRA: _____

Appreciations (for life, self, POWER, the people in your life, anything else):

```
┌─────────────────────────────────────────────────────────┐
│                                                         │
│                                                         │
│                                                         │
│                                                         │
│                                                         │
│                                                         │
│                                                         │
└─────────────────────────────────────────────────────────┘
```

Other reflection (thoughts, feelings, insights, musings, aha's, questions to ask on Q+As, etc.):

```
┌─────────────────────────────────────────────────────────┐
│                                                         │
│                                                         │
│                                                         │
│                                                         │
│                                                         │
│                                                         │
│                                                         │
└─────────────────────────────────────────────────────────┘
```

DATE: _____
TOPIC: _____
MANTRA: _____

Appreciations (for life, self, POWER, the people in your life, anything else):

Other reflection (thoughts, feelings, insights, musings, aha's, questions to ask on Q+As, etc.):

DATE: _____
TOPIC: _____
MANTRA: _____

Appreciations (for life, self, POWER, the people in your life, anything else):

Other reflection (thoughts, feelings, insights, musings, aha's, questions to ask on Q+As, etc.):

DATE: _____
TOPIC: _____
MANTRA: _____

Appreciations (for life, self, POWER, the people in your life, anything else):

```
┌─────────────────────────────────────────────────────────┐
│                                                         │
│                                                         │
│                                                         │
│                                                         │
│                                                         │
│                                                         │
│                                                         │
└─────────────────────────────────────────────────────────┘
```

Other reflection (thoughts, feelings, insights, musings, aha's, questions to ask on Q+As, etc.):

```
┌─────────────────────────────────────────────────────────┐
│                                                         │
│                                                         │
│                                                         │
│                                                         │
│                                                         │
│                                                         │
│                                                         │
└─────────────────────────────────────────────────────────┘
```

DATE: _____
TOPIC: _____
MANTRA: _____

Appreciations (for life, self, POWER, the people in your life, anything else):

Other reflection (thoughts, feelings, insights, musings, aha's, questions to ask on Q+As, etc.):

DATE: _____
TOPIC: _____
MANTRA: _____

Appreciations (for life, self, POWER, the people in your life, anything else):

Other reflection (thoughts, feelings, insights, musings, aha's, questions to ask on Q+As, etc.):

DATE: _____
TOPIC: _____
MANTRA: _____

Appreciations (for life, self, POWER, the people in your life, anything else):

```
┌─────────────────────────────────────────────────┐
│                                                 │
│                                                 │
│                                                 │
│                                                 │
│                                                 │
│                                                 │
│                                                 │
└─────────────────────────────────────────────────┘
```

Other reflection (thoughts, feelings, insights, musings, aha's, questions to ask on Q+As, etc.):

```
┌─────────────────────────────────────────────────┐
│                                                 │
│                                                 │
│                                                 │
│                                                 │
│                                                 │
│                                                 │
│                                                 │
└─────────────────────────────────────────────────┘
```

DATE: _____
TOPIC: _____
MANTRA: _____

Appreciations (for life, self, POWER, the people in your life, anything else):

Other reflection (thoughts, feelings, insights, musings, aha's, questions to ask on Q+As, etc.):

DATE: _____
TOPIC: _____
MANTRA: _____

Appreciations (for life, self, POWER, the people in your life, anything else):

Other reflection (thoughts, feelings, insights, musings, aha's, questions to ask on Q+As, etc.):

DATE: _____
TOPIC: _____
MANTRA: _____

Appreciations (for life, self, POWER, the people in your life, anything else):

Other reflection (thoughts, feelings, insights, musings, aha's, questions to ask on Q+As, etc.):

DATE: _____
TOPIC: _____
MANTRA: _____

Appreciations (for life, self, POWER, the people in your life, anything else):

```
┌─────────────────────────────────────────────────────────┐
│                                                         │
│                                                         │
│                                                         │
│                                                         │
│                                                         │
│                                                         │
│                                                         │
│                                                         │
└─────────────────────────────────────────────────────────┘
```

Other reflection (thoughts, feelings, insights, musings, aha's, questions to ask on Q+As, etc.):

```
┌─────────────────────────────────────────────────────────┐
│                                                         │
│                                                         │
│                                                         │
│                                                         │
│                                                         │
│                                                         │
│                                                         │
│                                                         │
└─────────────────────────────────────────────────────────┘
```

DATE: _____
TOPIC: _____
MANTRA: _____

Appreciations (for life, self, POWER, the people in your life, anything else):

Other reflection (thoughts, feelings, insights, musings, aha's, questions to ask on Q+As, etc.):

DATE: _____
TOPIC: _____
MANTRA: _____

Appreciations (for life, self, POWER, the people in your life, anything else):

Other reflection (thoughts, feelings, insights, musings, aha's, questions to ask on Q+As, etc.):

DATE: _____
TOPIC: _____
MANTRA: _____

Appreciations (for life, self, POWER, the people in your life, anything else):

Other reflection (thoughts, feelings, insights, musings, aha's, questions to ask on Q+As, etc.):

DATE: _____
TOPIC: _____
MANTRA: _____

Appreciations (for life, self, POWER, the people in your life, anything else):

Other reflection (thoughts, feelings, insights, musings, aha's, questions to ask on Q+As, etc.):

DATE: _____
TOPIC: _____
MANTRA: _____

Appreciations (for life, self, POWER, the people in your life, anything else):

Other reflection (thoughts, feelings, insights, musings, aha's, questions to ask on Q+As, etc.):

DATE: _____
TOPIC: _____
MANTRA: _____

Appreciations (for life, self, POWER, the people in your life, anything else):

Other reflection (thoughts, feelings, insights, musings, aha's, questions to ask on Q+As, etc.):

DATE: _____
TOPIC: _____
MANTRA: _____

Appreciations (for life, self, POWER, the people in your life, anything else):

Other reflection (thoughts, feelings, insights, musings, aha's, questions to ask on Q+As, etc.):

DATE: _____
TOPIC: _____
MANTRA: _____

Appreciations (for life, self, POWER, the people in your life, anything else):

Other reflection (thoughts, feelings, insights, musings, aha's, questions to ask on Q+As, etc.):

DATE: _____
TOPIC: _____
MANTRA: _____

Appreciations (for life, self, POWER, the people in your life, anything else):

Other reflection (thoughts, feelings, insights, musings, aha's, questions to ask on Q+As, etc.):

DATE: _____
TOPIC: _____
MANTRA: _____

Appreciations (for life, self, POWER, the people in your life, anything else):

Other reflection (thoughts, feelings, insights, musings, aha's, questions to ask on Q+As, etc.):

DATE: _____
TOPIC: _____
MANTRA: _____

Appreciations (for life, self, POWER, the people in your life, anything else):

Other reflection (thoughts, feelings, insights, musings, aha's, questions to ask on Q+As, etc.):

DATE: _____
TOPIC: _____
MANTRA: _____

Appreciations (for life, self, POWER, the people in your life, anything else):

```
┌─────────────────────────────────────────────────────────────┐
│                                                             │
│                                                             │
│                                                             │
│                                                             │
│                                                             │
│                                                             │
│                                                             │
│                                                             │
└─────────────────────────────────────────────────────────────┘
```

Other reflection (thoughts, feelings, insights, musings, aha's, questions to ask on Q+As, etc.):

```
┌─────────────────────────────────────────────────────────────┐
│                                                             │
│                                                             │
│                                                             │
│                                                             │
│                                                             │
│                                                             │
│                                                             │
│                                                             │
└─────────────────────────────────────────────────────────────┘
```

DATE: _____
TOPIC: _____
MANTRA: _____

Appreciations (for life, self, POWER, the people in your life, anything else):

Other reflection (thoughts, feelings, insights, musings, aha's, questions to ask on Q+As, etc.):

DATE: _____
TOPIC: _____
MANTRA: _____

Appreciations (for life, self, POWER, the people in your life, anything else):

```
┌─────────────────────────────────────────────────────────┐
│                                                         │
│                                                         │
│                                                         │
│                                                         │
│                                                         │
│                                                         │
│                                                         │
└─────────────────────────────────────────────────────────┘
```

Other reflection (thoughts, feelings, insights, musings, aha's, questions to ask on Q+As, etc.):

```
┌─────────────────────────────────────────────────────────┐
│                                                         │
│                                                         │
│                                                         │
│                                                         │
│                                                         │
│                                                         │
│                                                         │
└─────────────────────────────────────────────────────────┘
```

DATE: _____
TOPIC: _____
MANTRA: _____

Appreciations (for life, self, POWER, the people in your life, anything else):

Other reflection (thoughts, feelings, insights, musings, aha's, questions to ask on Q+As, etc.):

DATE: _____
TOPIC: _____
MANTRA: _____

Appreciations (for life, self, POWER, the people in your life, anything else):

```
┌─────────────────────────────────────────────────────┐
│                                                     │
│                                                     │
│                                                     │
│                                                     │
│                                                     │
│                                                     │
│                                                     │
│                                                     │
└─────────────────────────────────────────────────────┘
```

Other reflection (thoughts, feelings, insights, musings, aha's, questions to ask on Q+As, etc.):

```
┌─────────────────────────────────────────────────────┐
│                                                     │
│                                                     │
│                                                     │
│                                                     │
│                                                     │
│                                                     │
│                                                     │
│                                                     │
└─────────────────────────────────────────────────────┘
```

DATE: _____
TOPIC: _____
MANTRA: _____

Appreciations (for life, self, POWER, the people in your life, anything else):

Other reflection (thoughts, feelings, insights, musings, aha's, questions to ask on Q+As, etc.):

DATE: _____
TOPIC: _____
MANTRA: _____

Appreciations (for life, self, POWER, the people in your life, anything else):

Other reflection (thoughts, feelings, insights, musings, aha's, questions to ask on Q+As, etc.):

DATE: _____
TOPIC: _____
MANTRA: _____

Appreciations (for life, self, POWER, the people in your life, anything else):

Other reflection (thoughts, feelings, insights, musings, aha's, questions to ask on Q+As, etc.):

DATE: _____
TOPIC: _____
MANTRA: _____

Appreciations (for life, self, POWER, the people in your life, anything else):

Other reflection (thoughts, feelings, insights, musings, aha's, questions to ask on Q+As, etc.):